THE DAY I LEARNT TO BE BRAVE

How my mom taught me what
Brave really means

By: Kiera Barker

ABOUT THE AUTHOR

Kiera Barker is a Marine Mammal Specialist who is passionate about protecting the ocean and inspiring others to care for it too. She spends her days educating people about marine life and the importance of conservation. Kiera has always found peace and inspiration in the ocean. Growing up, she faced many challenges that shaped her into the strong and compassionate woman she is today. Her deep love for the sea and her personal journey of healing while recovering from a life-threatening surgery led Kiera to realize how powerful stories can be for helping children navigate life's challenges. In her free time, Kiera enjoys walking on the beach, going for a snorkel, and picking up seashells while listening to the calming sound of the waves. The ocean has always been a place of healing for her. The Day I Learnt to Be Brave is her debut children's book, written with love to honour her mother's strength during her battle with cancer. Through this story, Kiera hopes to comfort and empower young readers facing difficult times — reminding them that bravery comes in many forms, especially love. Kiera hopes to help little ones understand big emotions, discover their inner bravery, and feel a little less alone in the world.

ACKNOWLEDGEMENTS

"The Day I Learnt To Be Brave" is a heartfelt story about a little girl who discovers the true meaning of courage when she learns that her mommy has cancer. Through gentle words and tender illustrations, this book helps young children understand big feelings, scary moments, and how bravery can grow—even in the toughest times.

Written with love and honesty, and inspired by the Author's own journey, this story is a comforting guide for families facing difficult news. It opens the door for parents to talk to their children about illness, emotions, and the strength we find in each other.

DEDICATION

For my beautiful mother, Nearyna – Your strength lit the darkest days, your courage taught me how to stand tall. Thank you for showing me what it means to be truly brave. (I.L.U.T.A.T.O.F.A.D.C.S.H) This book is for you, and for every mother, daughter, and family learning to be brave together.

To my family and friends, your love and encouragement gave me the courage to bring this story to life.

To the doctors, nurses, and cancer warriors around the world – thank you for your strength and compassion.

And to every child who picks up this book: May you always remember that being brave doesn't mean being fearless – it means loving deeply, holding on tightly, and facing each day with hope in your heart.

Once upon a time, in a small town by the sea, there lived a little girl named Kiera. Her favorite place in the world was the beach.

Every weekend, Kiera and her mommy, Nina, would walk down the sandy path to the ocean. They would splash in the rockpools, find different kinds of shells, and build mermaid sandcastles together.

Every time they went to the beach, Kiera's mommy would braid her hair while they were sitting in their special beach tent (pink & yellow). It was flapping like a flag in the wind.

One Day, Kiera's mommy didn't swim. She sat in the tent, quiet and tired. Kiera noticed that her mommy's smile wasn't as big today.

That night, Kiera's mommy tucked Kiera into bed and held her close. "Sweetheart, I have something to tell you," Kiera's mommy whispered.

"Mommy is sick, and all this means is that I will need to visit the Doctor a bit more, and sometimes I might feel tired or look different. But no matter what, I will always love you".

Kiera's heart felt heavy, like a wave crashing down, but she held on tight to Mommy's hands. "Will you be okay?" she whispered.

"I'm going to try my very best," Mommy said, brushing Kiera's hair behind her ear. "And I need you to be brave with me. Can you do that?"

Kiera nodded her head slowly. She didn't feel brave, but she really wanted to be.

In weeks that followed, Mommy lost her hair, and sometimes she couldn't come to the beach. But Kiera still visited the rockpools and told her mommy stories about the seashells and the sea stars.

Mommy also had to wear a scarf on her head. Kiera helped pick out the best one for her mommy.

Some days, when Nina wasn't feeling well. Kiera missed her mommy's bedtime hugs and would hug her Dolphin Teddy tight.

Some days Kiera would build a blanket fort in the living room for them both to relax. Even when things felt a little scary, Kiera knew she needed to make her mom happy.

Kiera missed her mommy on the days she went to the hospital. But remembered what her mommy said: "Being brave doesn't mean you're not scared. It means you keep going, even when you are."

Kiera made her mommy a seashell necklace when her mommy had to go to the hospital. "This is for you, mommy; it will keep you safe," Kiera said while placing it over her mom's head. Nina smiled and said to Kiera, "You are my brave girl, Kiera!"

Kiera loved helping her mommy in the kitchen – especially when she was baking cupcakes. But when Nina wasn't feeling well, she would help her even more. Kiera would wash the vegetables and set the table, always trying to make her smile.

So Kiera decided to help her mommy feel better. She helped around the house with chores, especially cleaning her own room, so mommy didn't have to. And she would tell her mommy stories of the day she had at the beach on the days mommy couldn't go. Kiera would always bring back a special shell treasure from the beach for her mommy.

Kiera and Nina started a new tradition where they would paint. They loved to paint Bravery Rocks. Each one had a word – Hope, Strength, Love.

One day, Kiera decided to make a Bravery Jar. Each day, she'd write something brave she did or felt and add it to her jar.

One morning, while Kiera and Nina were sitting on the beach in their special tent watching a pod of Dolphins swim past, Nina smiled bigger than she had in weeks. While hugging Kiera, she recited a little poem: "When you feel small and shadows are near, remember, my love, I'm always right here. Brave isn't loud – it's quiet and true, it lives in your heart, and it shines out of you."

THE END

www.ingramcontent.com/pod-product-compliance
Lightning Source LLC
Chambersburg PA
CBHW041559040426
42447CB00002B/230